EXPLORERS AND COLONIZATION™

BARTOLOMEU DIAS

First European Sailor to Reach the Indian Ocean

JENNIFER SWANSON

Rosen
YA™
New York

Published in 2018 by The Rosen Publishing Group, Inc.
29 East 21st Street, New York, NY 10010

First Edition

Library of Congress Cataloging-in-Publication Data

Names: Swanson, Jennifer, author.
Title: Bartolomeu Dias : first European sailor to reach the Indian Ocean / Jennifer Swanson.
Description: New York: Rosen Publishing, 2018. | Series: Spotlight on explorers and colonization | Includes bibliographical references and index. | Audience: Grade 5 to 10.
Identifiers: LCCN 2016055886 | ISBN 9781508174950 (pbk. book) | ISBN 9781508174967 (6 pack) | ISBN 9781508174974 (library bound book)
Subjects: LCSH: Dias, Bartolomeu—Juvenile literature. | Explorers—Portugal—Biography—Juvenile literature. | Discoveries in geography—Portuguese—Juvenile literature. | Indian Ocean Region—Discover and exploration—Portuguese—Juvenile literature.
Classification: LCC G286.D53 S83 2018 | DDC 910.92 [B] —dc23
LC record available at https://lccn.loc.gov/2016055886

Manufactured in China

CONTENTS

AN EXPLORER FOR THE AGES

In the fifteenth century the European countries of England, Spain, Portugal, and France were searching for a way to trade directly with Asia and India. They wanted to purchase spices and goods that were not available in Europe, and sell them for great profit. However, traveling to these places on land routes was long, risky, and expensive. The king of Portugal decided that he would get around these problems by sending an explorer across the ocean. Bartolomeu Dias was that explorer. As the first Portuguese explorer to sail from the Atlantic Ocean to the Indian Ocean, Dias was one of the

most important explorers in history. His voyage around the tip of Africa and past the Cape of Good Hope paved the way for future explorers such as Vasco da Gama and Christopher Columbus.

Follow along with Dias as he battles huge storms, rough seas, dwindling supplies, and even a near mutiny on his historic trip to open up sea-going trade routes between Europe and Asia.

MEET BARTOLOMEU DIAS

Not much is known about the early life of Bartolomeu Dias. He was likely born around 1451 in Algarve, Portugal. In 1487, when he was in his early thirties, Dias was a member of the court of King John II of Portugal. Historians believe that he was in charge of the royal warehouses. He was also a sailing master, or navigator, for the *São Cristóvão*, a Portuguese man-o-war. A Portuguese man-o-war was a powerful warship capable of sailing long distances.

Dias most likely had a great deal of sailing experience in order to be appointed navigator. In 1481 he accompanied Diogo

d'Azambuja on an expedition to the Gold Coast of Africa. As navigator, Dias was responsible for planning the entire journey. He had to study current maps to determine the safest path.

FINDING A SEA ROUTE

European countries had come to depend on trade with Asia. They exchanged luxuries like silk and spices, but also widely used foodstuffs and raw materials. The trade routes brought many people together to create large cities which became cultural and artistic centers. People not only traded goods, but also ideas and religious beliefs.

King John II wanted to find a sea route in order to trade with the Far East. The land route that European countries had been using for this trade took a long time to travel over. In addition, the fall of the Mongolian Empire, and the takeover of the Chinese, made the land routes dangerous and

King John II of Portugal was determined to expand trade for his country. To do this, he supported efforts to find a trade route via the ocean that would connect Europe to Asia.

sometimes impassable. King John II's father had sent explorers to the Nile and the Congo looking for a way across Africa, but to no avail. So the king commissioned a new map to accomplish this goal. A cartographer monk in Venice, Fra Mauro, created it. He researched and concluded that the Indian Ocean was not a closed sea, but that the sea was below the bottom of Africa. A sea route to the East was found!

ON THE HUNT FOR PRESTER JOHN

King John II was not just interested in finding a trade route. He was also on the hunt to find the legendary Prester John. Tales said that Prester John ruled a large Christian kingdom in the East. Supposedly, his country was free from crime and overflowing with food and goods. Prester John's land was also said to have a river of pure gold. In the late twelfth century, a letter circulated Europe rumored to be from Prester John. The letter complained that Prester John's kingdom was under attack and asked for help from European

Christians. King John II, believing that the letter was true, sent two explorers to find Prester John. These men, Afonso de Paiva (ca. 1460–ca. 1490) and Pêro da Covilhã (ca. 1460–after 1526), took an overland route to Ethiopia, where Prester John was supposed to be living. At roughly the same time, John II also sent Bartolomeu Dias to locate Prester John. Dias, however, traveled by sea.

EQUIPPING HIS SHIP

Since his trip was expected to last more than sixteen months, Dias was given two *caravels*. A caravel was a fast, easily-steered sailing ship. Previous explorations proved that they were the safest ship for long journeys. Dias was also given an extra vessel to carry supplies. These supplies would be needed for the many months ahead. Caravels were used for long voyages since they were one of the few ships at the time that could sail into the wind. This allowed the ships to keep moving in the direction they wanted, even if the wind wasn't pushing them from behind.

Caravels were small, easily maneuverable ships designed by Portuguese shipbuilders and sailors for exploration along the African coast.

Dias picked the best pilots to go with him, men who were experienced sailors and highly regarded by the king. The supply ship was commanded by his brother, Pêro.

BON VOYAGE!

Dias's tiny flotilla, or group of ships, left Lisbon, Portugal in August 1487. Dias followed the route of fifteenth-century Portuguese explorer Diogo Cão, which kept the ships traveling close along the African coast. Cão had only made it as far as present-day Cape Cross, Namibia. Dias's fleet was headed much further than that, to Ethiopia. In preparation for the journey, Dias studied the current maps to learn as much as he could about the waters ahead.

The ships carried special limestone pillars, called *padrões*, that the Portuguese

This monument celebrated the successes of the Portuguese explorers' Age of Discovery. It is located in Lisbon, Portugal, the point where many of the explorers left on their journeys.

used to mark where they had landed. These markers would serve to guide future Portuguese sailors on their own trips. Dias followed the *padrões* that had been left by Diogo Cão, but only up to a certain point. After Dias passed by Cão's final marker, he had to rely on the stars and the land for navigation.

LEFT ALONG THE WAY

Dias's expedition included six Africans—two men and four women—who had been brought to Portugal by Diogo Cão. Dias's plan was to dress the Africans with silver, gold, and spices and drop them off at strategic points along the way. The Africans would then take the message of goodwill to the people who lived in the small villages. Dias hoped this would impress the native people and help them to understand that Portugal was a good and wealthy country. The Africans were also supposed to search for Prester John. One of the Africans died on the voyage,

An ancient shipwreck discovered in the sand of Skeleton Coast, Namibia. The hidden rocks off-shore made it difficult for ships to navigate and caused many ships to capsize.

but the others were sent onto land. The last two were left near Namibia, where Dias docked the supply ship guarded by a group of armed men. None of the Africans made it back to Portugal. Their messages and gold disappeared with them.

STORMS
AHEAD

Most of the information about what took place during Dias's voyage is lost. The actual records were kept in the castle of São Jorge, but the Lisbon earthquake in 1755 destroyed them. What little is known comes mainly from the limestone pillars that Dias left along the way. Scholars have also used the *Esmeraldo de Sito Orbis*, the route book of Duarte Pacheco Pereira to fill in details. Pereira was an explorer Dias rescued from Africa on his return trip.

Dias followed Cão's path fairly closely along the coast of Africa. By doing this, the waters would have been less violent. It

Portuguese sailors believed that going around Africa was a faster and safer way to get to Asia, where they could participate in the spice trade.

would also have been easier to find places to anchor at night. Eventually, Dias reached the end of Cão's path. The flotilla continued southward, but now the explorers were in uncharted territory. That meant that Dias could name each of the bays and inlets he encountered as he sailed past them.

By the end of December 1487, the ships had been at sea for four months. In order to avoid the harsh wind and heavy currents from the south, they had zigzagged along the coastline. It seemed like they weren't making much progress. In early January 1488, a massive storm blew up. Dias chose to steer his two ships away from the shore and out into the open Atlantic Ocean. It was a risky decision. What if they were blown out to sea and couldn't get back? They didn't have the supply ship to give them more food and water. The alternative was to be pushed into the rocky shore by the strong winds. This could damage the ship. Neither option seemed good, yet Dias had to choose. Using his great experience, he decided to head his ships out to sea. There, he would wait until the storm blew out. It turned out to be the best choice, one that changed history forever.

ROUNDING THE CAPE

The massive storm that caused Dias to turn his ships to a new course actually took the flotilla around the bottom tip of Africa. At the time, no one on board knew it, not even Dias himself. The weather was so bad they could barely see in front of them, and they could not see land at all. The crew became restless. Dias had gambled to save the ship by going into the open ocean. But had he instead doomed them to starvation?

After fourteen days at sea without seeing land, the temperature dropped, and it got very cold. Dias had sailed south into the Antarctic latitudes. He turned his ships

Bartolmeu Dias's ship rounded the Cape of Good Hope for the first time during a storm so violent and turbulent that they didn't even know they had passed it.

northward. On February 3, 1488 they landed on the eastern coast of Africa. The expedition had made it around the southernmost point of Africa. After sailing on for another 200 miles (322 kilometers), the weather became warmer. That's when they figured out that they were most likely on the eastern side of Africa.

ALMOST MUTINY

Sailing so long without an additional supply ship was becoming a problem for Dias's men. Their food and water were almost gone. Finally, they spotted land. The tired, hungry crew took the ship into a bay they named São Bras (today this is called Mossel Bay). Located about 300 miles (483 km) east of the Cape of Good Hope, this bay sits in the warmer waters of the Indian Ocean.

The chance to be off the ship and gather new supplies excited the crew. Their happiness was short-lived, however. Unfriendly natives pelted the ships with stones and arrows. One crew member,

Mossel Bay, South Africa, was the first bit of land that Dias's sailors saw after the violent storm. They must have been excited to see this barren beach.

possibly Dias himself, shot an arrow at them and killed a tribesman.

Dias wanted to push on along the coast, but this idea made the crew uneasy. Not only were they afraid of hostile tribes, but they were also plagued by exhaustion and hunger. The threat of mutiny against Dias was real.

HEADED HOME

In order to head off a mutiny, Dias decided to put his idea to push down the coast to a vote. He appointed a council of men to look at the expedition's options. The council agreed to sail on for three more days to see if they learned anything worthwhile, then turn around. Dias was not happy, but he agreed. They needed supplies, and the country was dangerous. But Dias also knew that King John II would be displeased if they didn't find Prester John.

The crew sailed on. They did not find any sign of Prester John, so they set out for home. Still, on the way back, Dias and his crew did achieve one of their goals. They

The Khoikhoi, natives of southwestern Africa, were known to be mostly nomadic farmers, which means that they traveled from place to place to find good land for their cattle to graze.

were finally able to see the southernmost point of Africa, which Dias named the Cape of Storms. The expedition stopped in Luderitz Bay to pick up their supply ship. They were surprised to learn that only three of the nine men left with the ship remained alive. The other six had been attacked and killed by the local tribe, the Khoikhoi.

AN UNHAPPY KING

With his flotilla together again, Dias headed home. In December 1488, more than sixteen months after they left, Dias and his crew returned. Triumphant crowds greeted the tired sailors, who had mapped more than 350 miles (563 km) of unexplored coastline. Despite the great reception from the people, King John II was unhappy. Dias had neither reached India, nor he had found Prester John.

When the maps were drawn up, King John changed the name of the Cape of Storms to the Cape of Good Hope.

While Dias had discovered a route which later opened up travel to India, he did not

This sign marks the point of the Cape of Good Hope which Bartolomeu Dias first rounded in 1488. It was placed as a symbol for all sailors who voyage through these seas.

receive much credit for it during his lifetime. He was never offered another job commanding an expedition.

Instead, Dias went to Guinea, where Portugal had established a gold-trading site, to live for several years.

THE SUCCESSFUL TRIP WITH DA GAMA

While Dias was in Guinea, King John II died. A new king, Manuel I, came to power. He recalled Dias to Portugal and asked him to build ships for the next big expedition to India. This expedition would be led by Vasco da Gama, a Portuguese nobleman and navigator. Dias supervised the building of two of the ships, the *São Gabriel* and the *São Rafael*. The *São Gabriel* became the flagship of da Gama's armada, or fleet of ships. In addition to the two ships built by Dias, da Gama also took a supply ship named the *São Miguel*.

In 1498, Vasco da Gama was the first European explorer to reach India via a sea route around Africa from Portugal.

Da Gama's trip lasted more than two years. He started by following the path along the African coast that Dias had traveled. Da Gama could easily see the *padrões*, the limestone pillars that Dias had left along his route. Dias accompanied da Gama to the Cape Verde Islands before he left the expedition to take over the fort at Mina, from which the Portuguese transported gold and slaves. Mina was located on the western cost of today's Ghana.

This image shows how the port of Calicut may have looked during the time the Portuguese explorers were living there.

Dias learned about trading at Mina. When he returned to Portugal, he brought a cargo of gold and slaves which were sold to pay for future expeditions.

Da Gama's trip was successful. Once he rounded the Cape of Good Hope, he made several stops along the eastern coast of Africa where Dias had also stopped. Then he went on farther than any European explorer had ever gone. Finally, in May 1498, da Gama reached Calicut, India. The ruler of Calicut was happy to trade with da Gama and supply him with a large cargo of spices. However, those traders who were already doing business with Calicut were not as thrilled to see da Gama. They demanded a big cut of his spices in return for the supplies da Gama desperately needed for his trip home.

A BETTER RECEPTION

Da Gama was welcomed back to Portugal in 1499 as a great hero. King Manuel was excited to learn of the treasures that could be found in India. He was anxious to set up a regular trade route between Portugal and India.

Soon after Vasco da Gama's voyage, King Manuel commissioned a new expedition. The king wanted to take advantage of the gold and spices reported to be in India. This new expedition would be much larger, however, and have a flotilla of thirteen ships. The leader was Pedro Álvares Cabral, but Dias was given command of one of the four

ships. Cabral, Dias, and the crew were to go back to India and also explore as far west as possible. They first sailed to Brazil, reaching it in 1500. Next, they traveled across the Atlantic Ocean towards South Africa. They were headed to India, where they hoped to get a good reception.

FINAL VOYAGE

Dias was one of the first explorers, along with Cabral, to discover Brazil. He was ordered to set out with a longboat, or a boat launched from a sailing ship that could be taken directly onto land. When he reached the land, Dias and his small crew interacted with the local tribes, who accepted them happily.

Dias was excited about his success in Brazil. Unfortunately, it did not last long. Near the Cape of Good Hope, which he had aptly named the Cape of Storms, the flotilla found themselves in a huge storm. All thirteen ships rocked along in the waves and

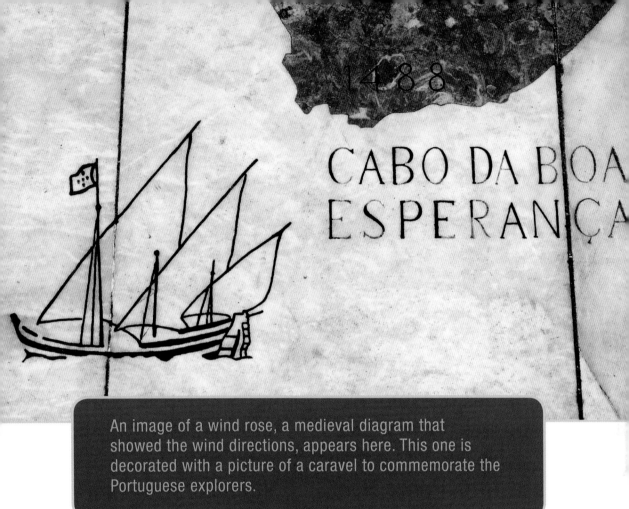

1488

CABO DA BOA
ESPERANÇA

An image of a wind rose, a medieval diagram that showed the wind directions, appears here. This one is decorated with a picture of a caravel to commemorate the Portuguese explorers.

wind. Four of the ships sunk, including the one commanded by Dias. Bartolomeu Dias went down with his ship. Despite its name, the Cape of Good Hope would continue to trouble many sailors for years to come.

LEGACY

Bartolomeu Dias was one of the unsung heroes of exploration. During his lifetime, he was not recognized for the significant achievement he made to world history. In 1410, Prince Henry the Navigator was determined to make Portugal the first country to round the tip of Africa and establish a trade route with India. Dias's voyage made that goal possible. Without Dias's contribution, the other Portuguese explorers would not have been able to follow. In fact, many scholars believe that Dias's voyage contributed to the establishment of the Portuguese Empire, which began in the late sixteenth century.

Bartolomeu Dias was a skilled navigator, ship builder, and leader. The discovery of much of the western African coast and the Cape of Good Hope was due to his efforts. He established relationships with some of the indigenous tribes which turned out to benefit Portugal. Without Dias's first exploration, Christopher Columbus, Vasco da Gama, and Pedro Álvares Cabral would not have been famous. In fact, Dias accompanied both da Gama and Cabral on their explorations, which followed the maps he made.

Memorials of Dias are found throughout Africa, including one at the Maritime Museum in South Africa. The Portuguese government built two navigational towers at the Cape of Good Hope. One of the towers was dedicated to Dias and the other to Vasco da Gama. A shipwreck found off the coast of Namibia in 2008 was originally thought to be Dias's. Ultimately this was proved false. However, one of Vasca da Gama's ships from his original voyage has been found.

Although Dias went on three successful explorations, he never did reach India. Despite this failure, his efforts led to the eventual development of trade with India. For that, he and his daring voyages will be long remembered.

GLOSSARY

caravel A small Spanish or Portuguese sailing vessel, usually lateen-rigged on two or three masts.

cartographer A person who makes maps.

flagship The most important ship in a group.

flotilla A group of ships moving together.

foodstuff A substance used or capable of being used as food.

goods Food and supplies needed by supply ships.

longboat A large boat carried by a sailing ship that is used to approach the shoreline.

mutiny A revolt or rebellion against an authority, especially by sailors against their officers.

navigator A person who practices, or is skilled in, the navigation of ships.

overland To travel across the land and not the sea.

padrões Limestone pillars left along the African shore by European explorers.

pillar An upright shaft or structure of stone that stands alone.

Portuguese man-o-war Ships used as the "heavy-guns" of the European fleet. They resembled galleons in design, but sported heavy fire-power with an average of sixty-five guns.

spices Dried fragrant plants used in cooking to add flavor.

uncharted territory An area that has been previously unexplored.

Bartolomeu Dias Museum Complex
1 Market Street
Mossel Bay, South Africa 6500
+27(0)44-691-1067
Website: http://diasmuseum.co.za
Five national monuments pertaining to Dias's first
    expedition are located on the museum grounds.

Canadian Museum of History
100 Laurier Street
Gatineau, Quebec K1A 0M8
Canada
(800) 555-5621
Website: http://www.historymuseum.ca
The Canadian Museum of History has many exhibits
    on the history of the great explorers from Europe
    to Asia.

The Mariners' Museum
100 Museum Drive
Newport News, VA 23606
(800) 581-7245
Website: http://exploration.marinersmuseum.org
The Mariners' Museum Library and Archives is
    the largest maritime library in the Western
    Hemisphere.

The Metropolitan Museum of Art
1000 5th Avenue
New York, NY 10028
(212) 535-7710
Website: http://www.metmuseum.org/toah/hd/expl
    /hd_expl.htm
The Europe and the Age of Exploration exhibit provides
    a wealth of information about European explorers.

The Navy Museum
Praça do Império 1400-206
Lisbon, Portugal
351-21-362-0019
Website: http://ccm.marinha.pt/pt/museu
The Navy Museum is a maritime museum dedicated to
    all aspects of the history of navigation in Portugal.

Websites

Because of the changing nature of internet links,
Rosen Publishing has developed an online list of
websites related to the subject of this book. This site
is updated regularly. Please use this link to access
this list:

http://www.rosenlinks.com/SEC/dias

Byers, Ann. *Pedro Álvares Cabral: First European Explorer of Brazil.* New York, NY: Rosen Publishing, 2016.

Cooke, Tim. *The Exploration of South America.* New York, NY: Gareth Stevens, 2013.

Curley, Robert. *Explorers of the Renaissance.* New York, NY: Britannica Educational Publishing, 2013.

Landau, Jennifer. *Vasco Da Gama: First European to Reach India by Sea*. New York, NY: Rosen Publishing, 2016.

Keller, Susanna. *The Age of Exploration Early American History.* New York, NY: Britannica Educational Publishing, 2016.

Pletcher, Kenneth. *The Age of Exploration: The Britannica Guide to Explorers and Adventurers.* New York, NY: Britannica Educational Publishing, 2013.

Pletcher, Kenneth. *Explorers of the Late Renaissance and the Enlightenment: The Britannica Guide to Explorers and Adventurers*. New York, NY: Britannica Educational Publishing, 2013.

Sheehan, Sean. *Ancient African Kingdoms.* New York, NY: Gareth Stevens, 2011.

BIBLIOGRAPHY

"The Ages of Exploration." Bartolomeu Dias. Mariners Museum. Retrieved October 12, 2016. http://exploration.marinersmuseum.org/subject/bartolomeu-dias.

Bar-Ilan, Meir. "Prester John: Fiction and History." Prester John: Fiction and History. Benson Idahosa University, 1996. https://faculty.biu.ac.il/~barilm/presjohn.html.

"Bartholomeu Dias." South African History Online. Retrieved October 12, 2016. http://www.sahistory.org.za/people/bartholomeu-dias.

Bio.com "Vasco da Gama Biography." A&E Networks Television. Retrieved October 12, 2016. http://www.biography.com/people/vasco-da-gama-9305736#early-years.

Crowley, Roger. *Conquerors: How Portugal Forged the First Global Empire.* New York, NY: Random House, 2015.

Department of Ancient Near Eastern Art. "Trade Routes between Europe and Asia during Antiquity." The Met's Heilbrunn Timeline of Art History. The Metropolitan Museum of Art, 2000. Retrieved October 12, 2016. http://www.metmuseum.org/toah/hd/trade/hd_trade.htm.

"History of the Caravel." History of the Caravel. Texas A &M University. Retrieved October 12, 2016. http://nautarch.tamu.edu/shiplab/01George/caravela/htmls/Caravel%20History.htm.

INDEX

About the Author

Jennifer Swanson has written numerous nonfiction titles for children. She got her love of history from her mother, who not only spent many hours reading about the explorers, but took her children to the places of their expeditions. Swanson has visited the sites of Marquette and Joliet landing in Green Bay, Wisconsin, as well as the Gateway Arch in St. Louis, Missouri, the spot where Lewis and Clark left on their journey. She would love to visit Portugal in the future to see where Bartolomeu Dias launched his first voyage.

Photo Credits